THE MODERN VEGAN

A TASTY NEW APPROACH TO HEALTHY EATING

PBP Publishing
4508 Atlantic Ave, Suite 241
Long Beach, CA 90805

ISBN 978-1-6319230-7-4

Cover design by Dymetra Pernell
Photography by Dymetra Pernell
Avatar created with Bitstrips

Contents

Dedication

I dedicate this book to my loving and devoted husband, Daric. You've been here to support me in all of my accomplishments. From helping me test recipes to sacrificing precious time to leave me to my creativity in the kitchen, and countless hours seclusion so I could focus. Thank you for always believing in me!

To my mother who has been one of the my greatest inspirations in the kitchen; you started it all. You've inspired me in ways unimaginable, and you never complained about my dishes that weren't so tasty; thank you. I love you.

To my grandmother Honey, you taught me the art of cooking. With you, I learned how to make a very simple dish come alive with flavor by simply adding different spices. Although there was no limit to the intricate dishes you could make, my favorite dish by you was a bowl of pinto beans and cornbread. I guess I've always been a vegan at heart.

And finally to my colleague Dr. Michael Imani, for being my guinea pig on a weekly basis (smile), and being honest enough to tell me flat out when something just did not taste good. Your input and "sophisticated palette" was the inspiration for many of the dishes in this book. Thanks for your continual support and encouragement.

To you, the reader; thank you for your purchase. I am hopeful that every dish will make you smile. Happy cooking!

Introduction

When clients or friends enquire about going vegan, their number one concern is breaking the bank by paying astronomical prices for food. Unfortunately this myth has captured the minds of many and caused plenty to turn away from a lifestyle that can improve their health and extend their lives. Are some foods more expensive? Absolutely. With the cost of living being sky high, and fast food restaurants offering dollar menus, it's very easy to lose perspective regarding dietary habits. While price should always be a consideration, there is one factor that is often overlooked when considering food and price; that factor is YOUR HEALTH. Sure, on the front end you're saving a few pennies, but at what cost? Obesity, cancer, type two diabetes, heart disease, and other chronic diseases plague the world right now. According to recents studies, out of pocket expenses for type two diabetes exceeds $15,000 per year. Talk about a budget killer. Here's the good news, each aforementioned diseases are categorized as "lifestyle diseases", meaning the attributing factors are diet and lack of exercise. With a few lifestyle adjustments each of them can be either reversed.

Vegan on a Budget was written with both your financial, and physical wellbeing in mind. Spending more to eat healthy does not always have to be the case. In the following pages we will discuss the organic craze that has taken America by storm and how to avoid marketing traps. We will discuss "health foods" vs. healthy foods. We will discuss a few simple tricks and tips on how to get the kids to make the transition and ween them off of the fast food junk craze. Most importantly, we will create and explore delicious recipes that will have you AND the kids going back for seconds. Enjoy!

About Me

I love food. I love to eat food. Food is my friend. However, over the years, food betrayed me in the worst way. My love affair with food caused me to tip the scales at 240lbs and my health to fail miserably. I had high blood pressure, severe food intolerances, and a myriad of issues. As a result of my health challenges and conducting lots of research, I decided to transition to a vegan lifestyle. I found the transition a bit challenging because though I knew my way around a kitchen after years of catering, I found myself missing certain comfort foods so I relapsed, over and over again. I'd go to vegan restaurants and the food was either unidentifiable, or full of soy, neither of which thrilled me. I was inspired. I understood that there were thousands of people just like me out there and something needed to be done. I began to create recipes that reminded me of mom's cooking, but wouldn't send me to an early grave (smile).

Once I made the full transition, within one month, I began to see drastic improvements in my energy level; I no longer suffered from brain fog, my attention span more than tripled, I was off of my blood pressure medication. I decided I would dedicate the rest of life to helping others achieve optimal health through food, after all, it IS medicine. I went back to school and became a certified health coach, and I am currently studying to become a naturopathic physician.

PANTRY LIST

I believe one of the most important tools in any kitchen is a well stocked pantry. A well stocked pantry is comprised of the "basics" or staples of every meal or snack you prepare. If you are missing just one spice or base ingredient, your dish well, just won't be the same. A pantry can contain as few or as many items as you wish. There are no rules here except for the ones you set. I have found that if you're on a budget it takes time to build a decent pantry, so if you do not have all of the items listed here please do not feel forced to run out and immediately purchase all of the items missing from your check list. There are a couple of things to consider when building a pantry. The first is practicality: before you purchase a new pantry ask yourself, "How often will I use this, and does this purchase make sense?" If you aren't going to make any dishes containing the spice saffron, is it really worth spending the astronomical price for this delicate spice just to complete your pantry list? I say not. The next thing to consider is how much to buy: Of course you save a bit of money by purchasing in bulk, but a major consideration is how ofter you will use this particular item, and whether the bulk of it will expire before you've had a chance to use it. When I go to the store to purchase potatoes, the 5 pound bag is always a great deal, but if I only need 2-3 potatoes from a 5 pound bag and the others go bad before I could use them, I've wasted about $3 of my hard earned money. That $3 could have gone toward other items on my shopping list.

Spices

Himalayan Sea Salt	Cloves (ground)
Seasoned Salt	Parsley
Black Pepper	Turmeric
Cayenne Pepper	Curry Powder
Red Pepper Flakes	Chili Powder
Granulated Garlic	Oregano
Granulated Onion	Basil
Cumin	Ground Ginger
Fennel Seed	Coriander
Cinnamon	Chipotle Powder
Whole Nutmeg	Bay Leaves
Allspice	Paprika
	Pure Vanilla Extract

Grains/Legumes

Brown Rice	Black Beans
Quinoa	Kidney Beans
Rolled Oats	White Beans
	Pinto Beans

Condiments

Yellow Mustard	Veganaise
Organic Shoyu	Chipotle Sauce
Organic Tamari	Tahini
Barbecue Sauce	Ketchup
	Dijon Mustard

Vegetables

Red Onions	Carrots
White Onions	Lemons
Red Potatoes	Limes
Gold Potatoes	Tomatoes
Garnet Yams	Cucumber

Canned Goods/Dried Fruit

Garbanzo Beans	Raisins
Tomato Paste	Cranberries
Diced Tomatoes	Dates
Coconut Milk	Figs
	Prunes

Oils/Vinegars

Ex. Virgin Olive Oil	Red Wine Vinegar
Walnut Oil	Distilled Vinegar
Sesame Oil	White Wine Vinegar
Coconut Oil	Non Hydrogenated
Balsamic Vinegar	Vegetable
Apple Cider Vinegar	Shortening

Nuts and Seeds

Raw Almonds	Macadamia Nuts
Sliced Almonds	Walnuts
Pecans	Sunflower Seeds
Pine Nuts	Flax Seeds
Raw Cashews	Raw Pumpkin
Unsalted Roasted	Seeds
Peanuts	Chia Seeds

Miscellaneous

Unsweetened	Unsweetened Dried
Cacao	Coconut Flakes
Light Agave	Fresh Nut Butters
Pure Maple Syrup	All Purpose Flour
Brown Sugar	Corn Meal
Demenara Sugar	Oat Flour
Almond Milk	Nutritional Yeast

Tools

From world renown chefs like Wolfgang Puck, to the home cook, everyone needs to have the proper tools. Having the proper tools at your disposal will make cooking simple, easy, and fun! There are a few things every kitchen should have:

High Speed Blender
Why choose a high speed blender? High speed blenders do what ordinary blenders cannot; they can make nut butters, grind coffee, grains, and break fruits and vegetables down to a cellular level, which aids in digestion. Blendtec and Vitamix have the market cornered on high speed blender. Which is better you ask? I actually like them both. The Vitamix seems to be able to take more of a beating. I've had to replace the jars for each of my Blendtecs but I love that I do not have to use a tamper to get a nice, smooth blend. I use the Blendtec to make my own oat flour, corn meal, and nut butters, and it has saved me tons of money.

Professional Grade Knives
You know the old adage, you can't miss what you've never had? Well I totally disagree. Many home chefs are unknowingly suffering because they lack proper knives; having a. There are a few must haves when it comes to knives:

Serrated Knife - ideal for cutting breads with crusty exteriors and soft foods like tomatoes.
Chef's Pairing Knife - perfect for doing detailed intricate work, and serves as a basic utility knife. The size of the blade (3 to 4 inches) allows for more control when dicing and chopping)
Chef's Knife - this knife is used for just about anything in the kitchen, from slicing to chopping it gets the job done with ease. When purchasing, look for one where the blade extends the entire length of the handle.

Food Processor
Let me start by saying I don't know what I'd do without my food processor. From slicing, to shredding, to chopping, to mixing, food processors can do it all. I have a Waring 2.5 quart processor. It came with every attachment I could dream of having, and was reasonably priced.

Types of cuts

There are countless types of cuts used in the culinary arts, and although it would be impressive that you knew them all, it just isn't necessary. The different types of cuts are used for various reasons; some for esthetics, others for uniformity in cooking, etc. I will cover some very basic cuts for you, as some of the recipes in this book call for different types of cuts. There are a few very basic cuts that are helpful to have in your arsenal. With each cut the knife is held in your dominate hand, and your free hand is used to steady the item you're cutting.

Julienne
A match stick type cut that is very thin, approximately 1/16th of an inch in diameter. To cut foods into julienne strips, first cut them lengthwise to 2 inches and 1/4 inch wide; stack them and slice stack into four sections.

Slice
Slicing requires that something be cut into strips or discs, usually 1/8 inch in thickness. Tomatoes are usually sliced before they are added to a sandwich.

Dice
A dice is achieved by starting with a slice and cutting is crossways to form a uniform square. Vegetables are typically diced before cooking. It is important when cooking the diced vegetables that you cut them as evenly as possible; this helps with things cooking uniformly. Other recipes like salsa require that vegetables are diced. Use a chef's knife or pairing knife when dicing.

Mince
To mince is simply a smaller dice. Garlic is an item that usually calls for mincing.

Rough Chop
A rough chop is just that, without any uniformity nor specific shape. Foods that would normally fall under the category of a rough chop include herbs.

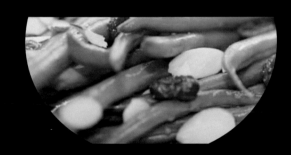

Starters

Chunky Guacamole

Prep Time: 10min I Total Time: 10min I Cost: $$

4 avocado, peeled, seeded, and diced
2 roma tomatoes, seeded and diced
1/2 small red onion, diced
juice from two medium limes

1/4 cup cilantro, roughly chopped
1 medium jalapeño, diced
1 clove garlic, minced (optional)
salt to taste

Add diced avocado, tomato, and onions, peppers, cilantro, and lime juice to a large mixing bowl and toss to coat. Add salt to taste and serve chilled with chips, or as a condiment to a main dish.

Prep Time: 10min | Total Time: 20min | Cost: $$

Roasted Corn Salsa

Ingredients

4 ears of yellow corn
2 medium Roma tomatoes, seeded and diced
1 small red onion, diced
1 small poblano pepper, seeded and diced
1 jalapeño, diced
1/2 cup cilantro, chopped
juice from 2 medium limes
1 tbsp extra virgin olive oil
kosher salt to taste

Directions

1. Preheat oven to 400°
2. Leave corn in husks and bake for 10 -15 minutes.
3. Brush poblano pepper with a bit of olive oil and place over an open flame and allow to char. Remove from heat and place in a plastic bag to cool.
4. Remove from oven and allow to cool.
5. Once corn has cooled, remove from husk with sharp knife.
6. Once the poblano has cooled, remove skin and seeds, and dice.
7. Place corn, poblano, and all remaining ingredients in a large mixing bowl and combine. Cover and refrigerate an hour before serving.

Grilled Veggie Skewers

Prep Time: 30min | Total Time: 40min | Cost: $$

Zucchini
Button mushrooms
Red onion
Cherry tomatoes
Yellow squash

Olive oil
Himalayan sea salt
Cracked black pepper
Soaked skewers

1. In a large bowl soak the skewers in water for 5 minutes and fire up grill.
2. Slice both the yellow squash and zucchini lengthwise, then chop into 1 inch cubes.
3. Remove stems from mushrooms and rinse.
4. Quarter the onion and set aside.
5. Assemble skewers in any way you'd like, using onion as a base.
6. Grill for 5 to 10 minutes, or until vegetables reach desired tenderness.
7. Remove skewers from grill and sprinkle with salt and pepper.
8. Serve warm.

Cheesy Kale Chips

Ingredients

2 bunches of kale
1 tbsp olive oil
1 tbsp fresh lemon juice

[for topping]
1 cup raw cashews
2 tbsp nutritional yeast
1/2 tsp Himalayan sea salt
1 tsp turmeric
1/4 cup red bell pepper
1/2 scotch bonnet pepper

Directions

1. Preheat oven to 250°
2. Rinse kale and spin dry, then rub down with olive oil, 1/4 tsp salt, and lemon juice and set aside.
3. In a food processor, combine cashews, remaining salt, nutritional yeast and turmeric and process until a powdered mixture forms.
4. Add bell pepper and scotch bonnet pepper to cashew mixture, and process until a thick and smooth paste forms.
5. Remove mixture from processor and massage kale, until evenly coated.
6. Evenly spread kale chips over baking sheet and bake until kale is dry and crispy.

Bruschetta

Prep Time: 10min | Total Time: 30min | Cost: $$

2 pints heirloom cherry tomatoes, diced and seeded
1 tbsp extra virgin olive oil
2 tbsp balsamic vinegar
2 cloves garlic, minced

6 basil leaves, rough chopped
1/4 tsp Himalayan sea salt
1/8 tsp cracked black pepper
1 french baguette, sliced

1. Preheat oven to 400°
2. Brush bread rounds with 2 tbsp olive oil and place on a cookie sheet.
3. Bake bread until golden brown and crispy.
4. Dice tomatoes and add to large mixing bowl.
5. Add garlic, olive oil, and chopped basil, and balsamic vinegar to tomatoes and toss to coat.
6. Season with salt and pepper to taste.
7. Cover and place in refrigerator for 20 minutes to allow flavors to merry.
8. Top toasted bread with 1 tbsp of tomato mixture and serve immediately.

Roasted GarlicHummus

Prep Time: 10min | Total Time: 10min | Cost: $

Ingredients

1 - 15oz can of garbanzo beans, drained and rinsed
2 cloves roasted garlic
1/3 cup water
1/4 tsp Himalayan sea salt
2 tbsp extra virgin olive oil
2-3 tbsp fresh lemon juice
1 tbsp tahini
1/4 tsp sumac powder (optional)

Directions

1. Place chickpeas, garlic, water, sea salt, olive oil, and lemon juice in a food processor. Process until mixture is smooth, scraping down the sides of bowl to ensure all ingredients are fully incorporated.
2. Transfer mixture to bowl and drizzle with olive oil.
3. Sprinkle with sumac and serve with pita chips

Cre"MINI"
Sliders

Prep Time: 5min | Total Time: 15min | Cost: $

crimini mushroom caps
extra virgin olive oil
Himalayan sea salt
cracked black pepper
slider buns

roasted garlic aioli (page
roma tomatoes, sliced thin
field greens

Preheat grill pan over medium high heat,
or heat outdoor grill to 400°. Toss
mushroom caps in olive oil and season
lightly with salt and pepper. Grill for 5
minutes per side.

Assemble sliders with remaining
ingredients and serve warm.

Prep Time: 5min | Total Time: 30min | Cost: $

Savory Sweet Potato Spears

Ingredients

2 lbs yams
4 tbsp extra virgin olive oil, separated
2 tbsp minced garlic
1 tsp Himalayan Sea Salt
cracked black pepper

*note, you can make this a sweet or savory dish. For a sweet version, salt and pepper with a cinnamon sugar mixture.

Directions

1. Preheat oven to 375°
2. Peel and cut yams to desired thickness. I usually go with 1/4 in to 1/2 in spears.
3. Rinse cut spears and towel dry.
4. Place in large bowl and toss with 2 tbsp extra virgin olive oil.
5. Place spears on a non stick baking sheet, or use parchment paper to line a baking sheet.
6. Bake for 20 - 25 minutes, or until spears are nice and crispy.
7. Remove from oven, toss with remaining olive oil, garlic, and season liberally with salt and pepper.

Pico de Gallo

Prep Time: 10min | Total Time: 10min | Cost: $

8 large Roma tomatoes, seeded and diced
1 medium red onion, diced
juice from 4 lemons
1/2 bunch cilantro, chopped

3 jalapeño pepper, diced
1 lb bag of tortilla strips

1. Combine tomatoes, onions, cilantro, lemon juice, and jalapeño in a mixing bowl and toss to coat.
2. Cover and chill in refrigerator for 1 hour.
3. Serve chilled with tortilla chips of your choice.

Smoothies

Looking for a quick boost? Smoothies if paired properly, can be extremely healthy and nourishing. The key to a healthy and nourishing smoothie is balance. Vegetables and berries should make up at least 50% of any smoothie. Why? Because your body converts fruits, vegetables, and just about everything you eat is converted into sugar (glucose). Since fruit is naturally high in sugar, you want to avoid overloading your bloodstream when taking it in. How can you do this? Fiber. Fiber slows down the rate at which the body absorbs sugar, and lessens the negative impact of overloading with sugars. Berries are acceptable fruits to eat in large quantities because they are loaded with fiber. Bananas are an exception to the rule. They are very high in fiber, but they are starchy, so we must treat them like a high sugar fruit. Vegetables are safe because they are naturally low in sugar. Have fun with these recipes, and create your own. Most of the smoothies listed here are

Banana Berry

1 very ripe medium banana
1 cup strawberries, frozen
1/2 cup blue berries, frozen
1/2 cup blackberries, frozen
1 cup coconut water

Place all ingredients in a high speed blender and blend until smooth. Adjust water to achieve desired consistency.

Green Machine

1 cup pineapple chunks, frozen
1 green apple
1 cup organic kale
1 cup spinach
1 cup coconut water

Place all ingredients in a high speed blender and blend until smooth. Adjust water to achieve desired consistency.

Mad Over Mangos

1.5 cup mango chunks, frozen
1.5 cup almond milk
1 handful of ice cubes
1 tsp agave or maple syrup

Place all ingredients in a high speed blender and blend until smooth. You can switch out the almond milk to suit your preference. I sometimes use coconut milk.

Citrus Berry

1 cup strawberries, frozen
1/2 cup blue berries, frozen
1/2 cup blackberries, frozen
1 large mandarine or orange, peeled and seeded
1 cup filtered water

Place all ingredients in a high speed blender and blend until smooth. Enjoy

Fiber Mania

1 cup raspberries
1 ripe pear
1/2 cup blueberries
1.5 cup coconut water
3 tbsp chia seeds

Place all ingredients in a high speed blender and blend until smooth. Adjust water to achieve desired consistency.

Peach Pleasure

1 cup diced peaches, frozen
1/2 cup strawberries, frozen
1 ripe banana
1 cup coconut water

Place all ingredients in a high speed blender and blend until smooth. Adjust water to achieve desired consistency.

Very Veggie

1 handful baby spinach
1 cup broccoli
1 medium ripe banana
1 small apple
1 cup coconut water

Place all ingredients in a high speed blender and blend until smooth. Adjust water to achieve desired consistency.

Beet It

1 small beet
1 cup pineapple
1 small apple
1 handful of ice cubes
1 cup unsweetened almond milk

Place all ingredients in a high speed blender and blend until smooth.

Pina Colada

1 cup pineapple chunks, frozen
1 very ripe medium banana
1.5 cup unsweetened coconut milk
1 tsp
1/2 tsp rum extract* optional

Place all ingredients in a high speed blender and blend until smooth. Adjust water to achieve desired consistency.

PB&C

1 medium ripe banana
2 tbsp organic creamy peanut butter
1 tbsp cacao
1 tbsp agave or maple syrup
1 cup plain cultured coconut milk

Place all ingredients in a high speed blender and blend until smooth. Adjust agave to suit your taste.

Orange Carrot Ginger Bliss

2 medium oranges, peeled
1/2 cup carrots
1 cup plain cultured coconut milk
1 tbsp fresh ginger
2 tsp maple syrup
1 handful ice of ice cubes

Place all ingredients in a high speed blender and blend until smooth. Enjoy

Tropical Delight

1 cup diced peaches, frozen
1 cup mango, frozen
1 cup pineapple chunks, frozen
1 ripe banana
1 cup coconut water

Place all ingredients in a high speed blender and blend until smooth. Adjust water to achieve desired consistency.

Salads

Salads are probably the most recognized meals in vegan cuisine. What most may not understand is the importance of eating fresh greens on a daily basis. Greens are probably the single most important food you can eat to help improve your health. Greens are loaded with vitamins, minerals, fiber, protein, and antioxidants, and are celebrated for their ability to help fight against diabetes, heart disease, cancer, and other chronic diseases. Kale is the queen of all greens; it's packed with vitamins A, C, and K. Collard, turnip, and mustard greens follow kale very closely in nutritional value. I strongly encourage you to fit at least three servings of greens into your daily diet; your heart, arteries, and blood cells will love you for it.

Field of Greens

Ingredients

1 4oz bag of baby greens
1/4 cup dried cranberries
1/4 raw sunflower seeds
1/4 hemp seeds
1/2 cup strawberries (or any seasonal berry)
1/4 cup White Balsamic Strawberry
Lemongrass Vinaigrette (page

Directions

1. Preheat oven to 350°
2. In a large saucepan over medium heat, combine water, lemon juice, and sugar, and cook until sugar dissolves
3. Add berries and reduce heat to a simmer.
4. Add flour and smart balance and cook until mixture begins to thicken (approximately 3 minutes)
5. Remove from heat, pour into ramekins until 3/4 full, and allow mixture to cool.
6. Cover each ramekin with pie crust; cut slits in top of crust so heat can escape while baking
7. Sprinkle crust with sugar
8. Bake at 350° for 20 minutes, or until crust is golden brown.
9. Remove from oven and allow to cool

Kale Salad

Prep Time: 10min | Total Time: 10min | Cost: $$

2 bunches of kale, rinsed and spun dry
1/2 pint cherry tomatoes
1/2 small red onion, sliced
1 red bell pepper, julienned
juice from 2 lemons
3 tbsp extra virgin olive oil

1/2 tsp Himalayan sea salt
1/2 tsp cracked black pepper
1/2 cup cranberries
1 cup walnuts, roughly chopped
1 medium Haas avocado

1. Soak kale in cold water for 5 minutes.
2. Remove stems from kale and spin in a salad spinner until kale is fairly dry.
3. Massage kale with lemon juice, olive oil, and salt until tender, but not wilted.
4. Slice cherry tomatoes in half and add to kale mixture.
5. Add bell pepper, avocado, nuts, cranberries, and pepper, and toss for two minutes or until well combined.
6. Enjoy!

Marinated Broccoli Salad

Prep Time: 30min | Total Time: 45min | Cost: $$

Ingredients

1 pound of broccoli crowns, chopped
1 small red onion, sliced
1 pint grape tomatoes, halved
1 cup copped walnuts
1/2 cup dried cranberries
2 tbsp dijon mustard
2 tbsp extra virgin olive oil
2 tbsp fresh squeezed lemon juice
4 tbsp white balsamic vinegar
1 tbsp honey
1/2 tsp Himalayan sea salt
pinch of cracked black pepper

Directions

1. In a bowl whisk together mustard, white whine vinegar, honey, sea salt, and pepper until well blended.
2. Slowly drizzle in olive oil while whisking mixture and set aside.
3. Separate broccoli crowns from stems and chop crowns into bite sized pieces, and thinly slice stalks. Place into large mixing bowl.
4. Place tomatoes, onions, walnuts, and cranberries in mixing bowl with broccoli and toss with honey-dijon vinaigrette.
5. Refrigerate salad for one hour.
6. Serve cold.

Chopped Apple Salad

Prep Time: 30min | Total Time: 45min | Cost: $$

[For Salad]
3 Pink Lady Apples
3 Granny Smith Apples
1 4oz bag of baby spinach
1- 4oz bag of mixed greens
1 1/2 c candied walnuts (page
2 c grapes, halved
Lemon juice

[White Balsamic Vinaigrette]
1/4 cup white balsamic vinegar
1 tbsp Dijon mustard
1 tsp honey
1/4 cup extra virgin olive oil
Salt and pepper to taste

Slice apples into bite sized pieces and toss in lemon juice. Place all ingredients for salad in large mixing bowl and set aside.
For the vinaigrette, whisk together white balsamic vinegar, mustard, salt and

pepper until smooth, then slowly drizzle in olive oil while whisking rapidly.
Toss salad with vinaigrette and serve immediately.

Prep Time: 30min | Total Time: 45min | Cost: $$

Mock Tuna Salad

Ingredients

2 pounds of carrots
1 cup celery, diced
1 cup red onion, diced
1/4 cup dulse flakes
2.5 cups vegan mayonaise

Directions

1. Juice carrots and place pulp in large mixing bowl.
2. Add celery, onion, dulse, and vegan mayonnaise and mix until thoroughly combined. Mixture should be moist, but not loose. You can adjust the moisture by either adding more mayonnaise, or carrot juice.
3. Place in airtight container and place in refrigerator for at least one hour so flavors marry.
4. Serve on toasted bread with lettuce, tomato, and onion.

Potato Salad

Prep Time: 30min | Total Time: 45min | Serves 20

5 pounds red potatoes, cubed
1 tbsp Himalayan sea salt
2 tsp cracked black pepper
1 - 32oz jar of vegan mayonnaise
1 bunch green onions, chopped
2 tbsp yellow mustard

*reserve 1/2 cup green onions for garnish.
*potato salad is best if consumed the same day it was prepared.

1. Bring large pot of water to a boil
2. Wash potatoes and cut into 1/2 inch cubes and add to boiling water. Boil until fork tender.
3. Drain potatoes and let cool.
4. Once potatoes are cool, place in large mixing bowl and season with salt and pepper.
5. Add remaining ingredients and mix until thoroughly combined.
6. Top with garnish, cover and refrigerate one hour.
7. Serve chilled.

Prep Time: 30min | Total Time: 45min | Serves 3-4

Quinoa Salad

Ingredients

1 cup dry quinoa
2 cups water or vegetable broth
1 cup chopped red onion
1 cup whole kernel corn
2 medium roma tomatoes, seeded and diced
1/2 cup toasted pine nuts
juice from 2 lemons (1/2 cup)
2 tbsp extra virgin olive oil
2 tbsp white wine vinegar
salt and pepper to taste
2 avocados peeled, seeded, and diced for garnish.

Directions

1. Bring 2 cups of water to a boil, add quinoa, reduce heat, and cover. Allow to simmer for 20 minutes and remove from heat. Allow quinoa to cool.
2. In a large bowl whisk together lemon juice, olive oil, and vinegar until combined.
3. Add quinoa and remaining ingredients to bowl and toss to coat.
4. Cover with saran and chill for one hour before serving.
5. Garnish with avocado before serving.

Marinated Vegetable Salad

Prep Time: 15min | Total Time: 1 hr 15min | Cost: $$

1 English cucumber, peeled, seeded, and diced
1 pint cherry tomatoes, halved
1 small red onion, thinly sliced
1 bunch blanched asparagus spears

1 large red bell pepper, sliced
1/4 cup white wine vinegar
1/4 cup extra virgin olive oil
1 tbsp minced garlic
2 tbsp italian seasoning (page

1. In a medium bowl whisk together olive oil, vinegar, minced garlic, and italian seasoning. Cover and refrigerate for 30 minutes.
2. Bring two quarts of water to a boil. Cut and discard the bottom third of the asparagus spears, and add tops to boiling water. Boil for 3 minutes.
3. In a large bowl, add 1 quart of water and 3 handfuls of ice cubes. Remove asparagus from boiling water and add to ice water to stop the cooking process.
4. Add all vegetables to large mixing bowl and drizzle with marinade. Toss to coat.
5. Place in refrigerator and chill for 1 hour.
6. Serve cold.

Prep Time: 30min | Total Time: 1 hr 15min | Serves 8

Lentil Salad

Ingredients

1 cup dry brown lentils
2 cups water or vegetable broth
1 tsp kosher salt
1 bay leaf/ 1 sprig of thyme (1/2 tsp)
1/4 cup red onion, diced
1 large carrot, peeled and diced
1 stalk celery, diced
1 handful flat leaf parsley
1/4 cup red bell pepper, diced
1 garlic glove, minced
1/4 fresh lemon juice
2 tbsp extra virgin olive oil
salt and pepper to taste

Directions

1. Bring 2 cups of water to a boil, add lentils, reduce heat, and cover. Allow to simmer for 15 minutes or until lentils are tender. Add more broth, if needed. Remove from heat and allow lentils to cool.
2. In a large bowl whisk together lemon juice and olive oil.
3. Add lentils and remaining ingredients to bowl and toss to coat.
4. Cover with saran and chill for one hour before serving.
5. Serve chilled.

Pasta

Pasta is filling, delicious, and nutritious. Like any other complex carbohydrate, too much of it can pack on the pounds. Add lots of green veggies like broccoli and spinach to balance out pasta dishes. Whole wheat pasta is a great alternative for that extra boost of fiber and whole grains.

Roasted Veggie Pasta

Prep Time: 10min | Total Time: 35min | Serves 3-4

1/2 pound asparagus tips
1 medium yellow squash, diced
1 large zucchini, diced
2 pints grape tomatoes
1 small red onion, cut into eighths
2 cloves garlic

1/4 cup basil leaves, chopped
1/4 cup plus 2 tbsp extra virgin olive oil
1 lb bow tie pasta
4 tsp salt divided
2 tsp cracked black pepper

1. Preheat oven to 400°. Place asparagus, squash, zucchini, tomatoes, onion, and whole garlic gloves on a baking sheet. Season with salt and pepper and drizzle with 2 tbsp olive oil. Toss to coat and roast for 10 minutes.

2. In a large pot boil pasta with two tsp salt until tender, but not overcooked (approx 8 - 10 min). Drain pasta and rinse.
3. Toss pasta, roasted vegetables, olive oil, basil, salt, and pepper.
4. Serve warm

Angel Hair Pasta and Tomatoes

Ingredients

1 pound angel hair pasta

2 tbsp olive oil

2 garlic cloves, minced

3 medium roma tomatoes, seeded and diced

1/4 cup basil, chopped

2 tbsp fresh oregano

4 tsp Himalayan sea salt, divided

Directions

1. Cook pasta al-dente according to package instructions. Drain and set aside. Reserve 1/2 cup liquid.
2. In a medium sauce pan heat oil over medium heat and add garlic and tomatoes and sauté for two minutes.
3. Add pasta and reserved water and cook for 3 minutes.
4. Add in basil and oregano.
5. Season with salt and pepper to taste.
6. Serve warm.

Spinach Stuffed Shells

Prep Time: 40min | Total Time: 45min | Serves 6-8

20 jumbo shells
1 tsp fresh oregano, chopped
1 tsp fresh thyme, chopped
1- 10oz box of frozen spinach, thawed and drained
1 cup vegan ricotta (page ???)

1 cup bechamel sauce (pg. ???)
salt and pepper to taste
2/3 cup vegan parmesan cheese
1 recipe marinara sauce (pg. ???)

1. Preheat oven to 475°
2. Boil shells in 5 to 6 quarts of water for 6 to 8 minutes until al dente. Rinse under cool water and set aside.
3. Thaw spinach and drain.
4. Mix spinach with ricotta
5. Stuff shells with 1 to 2 tsp of the ricotta filling and line the bottom of a glass or porcelain dish with béchamel and 3/4 cup marinara sauce and place stuffed shells face up in sauce. Cover tightly with foil and bake for 15 minutes.
6. Uncover, sprinkle with vegan parmesan and bake for another 10 to 12 minutes.
7. Use remaining marinara to sauce the plates.

Macaroni and Cheese

Ingredients

16oz elbow macaroni

3 tbsp vegan butter

2 tsp seasoned salt, plus salt to taste

1 tsp granulated garlic

1 tsp granulated onion

1/4 tsp cayenne pepper

1/4 tsp sweet paprika

1 cup coconut milk

1 large yukon gold potato, peeled and diced

1 large carrot, peeled and diced

3/4 cup hot water (from boiled vegetables)

1/2 cup raw cashews

2 tbsp plus one teaspoon nutritional yeast

1 tbsp fresh lemon juice

salt and pepper to taste

Directions

1. Boil macaroni in salted water for 8 to 10 minutes, rinse and drain. While macaroni is still hot, mix in vegan butter, seasoned salt, granulated garlic, cayenne pepper, and paprika.
2. In a separate pot, boil potatoes and carrots until tender. Strain veggies and reserve 3/4 cup of the remaining liquid.
3. In a blender, add veggie, reserved water, coconut milk, lemon juice and sautéed onions and blend until smooth.
4. Pour sauce over noodles and stir until combined and serve immediately.

Spaghetti with Marinara

16 oz spaghetti, prepared per package instructions
[Marinara Sauce]
8 medium tomatoes, peeled, seeded, and diced.
2 tbsp extra virgin olive oil
2 cloves garlic, minced

1 medium red onion, chopped
6 oz tomato paste
1/4 cup dry red wine (optional)
1 tbsp sugar
1 tsp dried oregano
3 basil leaves, chopped
1 tsp salt

1. Prepare spaghetti per package instructions, drain and rinse.
2. In large sauce pan, heat oil over medium to high heat and sauté the onions and garlic until onions begin to brown. Add the remaining ingredients and bring to a boil. Reduce heat and simmer until sauce thickens, approximately 35 minutes, stirring occasionally.
3. Top spaghetti with sauce and serve warm.

Penne Pasta with Savory Cream Sauce

Ingredients

1 lb box of penne pasta, cooked

1 recipe of cream sauce (page

1 large broccoli crown, cut into bite sized pieces

6 - 7 sun dried tomatoes in oil, sliced

1/2 cup red bell pepper, diced

1 tbsp red pepper flakes

2 tsp Himalayan sea salt

Directions

1. Cook pasta according to package instructions. Meanwhile, in a large saucepan bring 3 quarts of water to a boil and add broccoli. Cover and let cook for 4 minutes and drain rinse under cold water for one minute. Set aside.
2. In a large saucepan bring cream sauce to a boil. Add in penne pasta, broccoli, sun dried tomatoes, salt, and red pepper flakes. Reduce heat and simmer for five minutes.
3. Serve warm.

Gnocchi with an Herbed Butter Sauce

Prep Time: 30min | Total Time: 45min | Serves 4-6

16 oz package of gnocchi
4 tbsp vegan butter
1 tsp fresh thyme
1 tsp fresh oregano

5 fresh basil leaves, chopped
5 sun-dried tomatoes, packed in oil
1 tsp garlic, minced
1 tsp salt

1. Add a tablespoon of salt to a large pot of water and bring to a boil.
2. Add gnocchi to boiling water and cook until they begin to float. Cook an additional 4 minutes and remove from water using a slotted spoon.
3. In a large sauce pan, melt butter, add herbs, sun-dried tomatoes, garlic, and herbs and cook for 1 minute, then add gnocchi. Season with salt and pepper.
4. Cook for an additional 4 minutes and serve immediately.

Sandwiches and Wraps

Sandwiches and wraps are quick and easy ways to fill up on the go. I usually make wraps when I'm going to be out for a while; they store really well in cool temps, and are portable, which makes them very convenient. There are no rules with wraps. Find your favorite veggies and wrap them up in a collard green leaf or spinach tortilla.

The Perfect Veggie Wrap

Prep Time: 15min | Total Time:35min | Serves 4

Ingredients

4 large tortilla wraps
2 cups hummus (pg. 6)
3 - 4 peeled carrots, julienned
2 medium cucumbers, julienned
1 small red onion, sliced
1 large red bell pepper, julienned
1 large orange or yellow bell pepper, julienned
4 oz. baby spinach
2 medium roma tomatoes, seeded and diced

Directions

1. Using a utility knife, julienne cucumbers, bell pepper, and carrots.
2. Lay tortillas on a flat surface and evenly spread 1/2 cup hummus over the entire surface.
3. Lay out 1 - 2 handfuls of spinach in the center of the tortilla, followed by a handful of each of the remaining veggies.
4. Roll up into a burrito and enjoy.

Raw Collard Wraps

Prep Time: 30min I Total Time: 45min I Serves 8-10

[Wraps]
1 bunch raw collard greens, washed and stems removed
apple cider vinegar
1 large red bell pepper
1 large red onion
1 large cucumber, seeded
2 avocados
1 cup shredded carrots

2 cups cooked quinoa
1 pint grape tomatoes, halved

[for dipping sauce]
1/2 cup whole grain mustard
1 tbsp fresh squeezed lemon juice
1 tbsp white wine vinegar
1 tbsp honey
salt and pepper to taste

Wash greens, pat dry with a paper towel, and remove stems. Pour a bit of apple cider vinegar into a bowl and use a pastry brush to apply to the collard leaves. Stack the leaves flat and place in an oversized ziplock bag and allow to sit for one hour or overnight. Remove leaves from bag; they should be pliable and tender. Layer a bit of each vegetable, and 3 tbsp of cooked quinoa in each leaf, and roll, tucking the edges in as you go (like a burrito). For dipping sauce, add all ingredients to a medium mixing bowl and use a whisk to combine. Serve wraps with sauce on the side. Enjoy

Yummy Lettuce Wraps

Prep Time: 30min | Total Time: 45min | Serves 4

1 head of iceberg lettuce, cut in half
1 can great northern beans, drained and rinsed
1 can bamboo shoots, chopped
1 cup walnuts, soaked
1 tbsp garlic-ginger paste

3 tbsp tamari or soy sauce
1 tbsp sesame oil
shredded carrots, cilantro, and green onion, for garnish
Chili sauce for dipping

1. Soak walnuts in water for 1hr, rinse, drain, and place in food processor with bamboo shoots and pulse for 10 seconds.
2. In a separate mixing bowl, whisk together garlic-ginger paste, tamari, and sesame oil until blended.
3. Add beans and walnut mixture to the soy mixture and toss to coat.
4. Transfer mixture to saucepan over low to medium heat for 5 minutes.
5. Spoon mixture into lettuce cups and top with carrots, cilantro, and green onions.
6. Chili sauce can be purchased at your local grocer.

The Stack

Ingredients

Cucumbers, sliced lengthwise and patted dry
Tomatoes, sliced
Red onion, sliced
Red bell pepper, sliced
Dill Pickle chips
Mixed baby greens
Mustard
Vegan Mayo
Salt
Pepper

Directions

1. Slice and prep vegetables and set aside for sandwich preparation.
2. Use 1/2 tbsp vegan mayo and apply to one slice of bread.
3. Use 1/2 tbsp yellow mustard and apply to second slice of bread.
4. Assemble sandwich by stacking sliced vegetables on one slice of dressed bread, and top with salt and pepper, and top with second piece of bread.

*Note: Be sure to use a high quality wheat bread to prevent sandwich from becoming soggy. This sandwich can also be assembles on a french roll.

Entrees

The heart of most meals for vegans are some form of bean, grain, and or/ legume.
Generally loaded with protein and fiber, these dishes are both filling and satisfying. Pair any

Aloo Gobi

Ingredients

1 head small head of cauliflower

5 medium to large yukon gold potatoes

6 roma tomatoes, quartered, plus 3 more

1 medium yellow onion, peeled and quartered

2 serrano peppers, stems removed

1 inch piece of ginger, peeled

3 garlic cloves, peeled

Type to enter text

Directions

Dice potatoes into 1 inch cubes and cut cauliflower into florets and set aside. Add 6 tomatoes and the next 4 ingredients to a food processor and blend until smooth. Meanwhile, heat 2 tbsp of olive oil to a large sauce pan over medium heat and add cumin seeds. Cook until seeds begin

Savory Black Beans

Prep Time: 30min I Total Time: 45min I Serves 8

2 cups dry black beans, rinsed
2 tbsp seasoned salt
2 tbsp granulated onion
2 tbsp granulated garlic
1 tbsp oregano
1 tbsp ground cumin
1 tsp red pepper flakes
6 - 8 cups filtered water

1. Place all ingredients in a crockpot and stir to combine. Turn crockpot on high and cook for 4 - 6 hours on high, or until beans are tender. Start with 6 cups of water and add more if needed.

Prep Time: 10min I Total Time: 35min I Serves 8

Lentil Soup

Ingredients

1 - 16oz bag of brown lentils
2 medium yukon gold potatoes, peeled and diced
1/2 cup carrots, diced
1/2 cup celery, diced
1/2 cup yellow onion, diced
2 tbsp extra virgin olive oil
2 tsp Himalaya sea salt
1 tsp black pepper
1 tsp oregano
2 sprigs thyme
1 bay leaf

Directions

1. In a large pot over medium heat sauté carrots, celery, and onions in olive oil for 4 minutes.
2. Add water and remaining ingredients to pot, turn up heat, and bring to a boil.
3. Reduce heat and simmer for 25 to 30 minutes or until lentils are tender and potatoes are soft.
4. Remove sprigs of thyme and bay leaf and serve warm.

Smokehouse Chili

1 cup each, kidney beans, black beans,
great northern beans (soaked)
1/2 yellow onion, diced
6 roma tomatoes
2 - 15oz cans diced tomatoes
2 tbsp chili powder
1 tbsp cumin
1 tbsp ground chipotle powder

2 tsp black pepper
2 tbsp turbinado sugar
2 tsp Himalayan sea salt
2 cloves garlic, minced
1/2 cup red bell pepper, chopped
1 tsp oregano
1/2 tsp thyme
6 - 8 cups water

1. Measure out 1 cup of each bean and
   soak in water overnight.
2. Drain and rinse soaked beans.
3. Place all ingredients in a crockpot and
   stir to combine. Turn crockpot on high
   and cook for 4 - 6 hours on high, or

until beans are tender. Start with 6
cups of water and add more if needed.

Prep Time: 10min | Total Time: 5hrs 10min | Serves 10-12

Southern Black Eyed Peas

Prep Time: 5 min. I Total Time: 8 hours I Serves 4-6

Ingredients

2 cups of dry black eyed peas
5 cups water plus more for soaking
1/4 cup yellow onion, diced
1 tbsp seasoned salt
1/2 tsp granulated garlic
1/2 tsp cracked black pepper

Directions

1. Place peas in an airtight container and soak in 6 cups purified water overnight.
2. Drain and rinse peas and set aside.
3. Add peas, fresh water, and seasonings to a large pot and bring to a boil.
4. Cook peas until tender and add more water if needed while cooking.
5. Serve warm with jalapeño cornbread

Black Bean Burger with Sweet Hoisin Glaze

2 cups cooked black beans, drained
2 cups cooked brown rice
2 garlic cloves, minced
1 small beet, roasted and diced (pg. 72)
1/3 cup red onion, minced
8 dried figs, chopped
5 dried prunes, chopped
1 tbsp sweet hoisin sauce (page

1 tsp chili powder
1 tsp ground cumin
1 tsp Himalayan sea salt
1/2 tsp black pepper
1 jalapeño, seeded and diced
1/3 cup oat flour
2 tbsp extra virgin olive oil, divided
3 tbsp bbq sauce

1. In a large mixing bowl combine all ingredients and mix until well combined.
2. Heat 1 tbsp olive oil in pan.
3. Scoop 1/2 cup black bean mixture with an ice cream scoop and place in skillet. Flatten out ball with spatula and pan fry for 2 to 3 minutes on each side and dress with glaze.
4. Serve on toasted bun.

Prep Time: 10min | Total Time: 5hrs 10min | Serves 6

Chili Smoke Burger

Ingredients

2 cups cooked black beans
2 cups cooked brown rice
1/4 yellow onion, minced
1 clove garlic
1 tbsp bbq seasoning
2 tbsp bbq sauce
1 tsp liquid smoke
2/3 cup oat flour

Topping
Chili (page 40)
Chopped onions

Directions

1. In a large bowl combine all ingredients. Once fully incorporated, add half the mixture to a food processor and process mixture until most of the product has been broken down.
2. Reincorporate mixture into the bowl and thoroughly combine.
3. Heat 1 tbsp olive oil in a cast iron skillet or other non stick pan over medium-high heat. Use ice cream scooper to scoop out black bean mixture. Flatten ball into a patty and pan fry for 2-3 minutes per side.
4. Add to toasted bun, top with chili, lettuce tomatoes, onions, and mustard and enjoy.

Sides and Small Plates

Green Beans and Almonds

1 lb. fresh green beans, whole
1/2 cup blanched almonds, slivered
1/2 cup dried cranberries
1 garlic clove, minced
1 tbsp extra virgin olive oil
salt and pepper to taste
large bowl of ice water (ice bath)

Bring large pot of water to boil, add green beans, and cook for 3 minutes. Remove green beans from boiling water and place in ice bath (1 cup of ice to 2 cups water) to stop cooking. In a large saucepan, heat olive oil on medium heat, then add garlic and almonds cook for 2 minutes, add green beans, cranberries, salt, pepper, and toss for 2 minutes. Remove from heat and serve warm.

Sautéed Spinach

10oz. baby spinach
1 tbsp vegan butter
2 tsp extra virgin olive oil
2 tbsp shallot, minced
1 tsp garlic, minced
salt and pepper to taste

In a large skillet, melt butter then add olive oil and shallot. Cook until shallot is tender, about 2 minutes. Add the spinach and cook until spinach is wilted, and bright green, constantly stirring. Season with salt and pepper to taste. Serve warm.

Candied Yams

3 lbs garnet yams, peeled and cubed
2 cups granulated sugar
3 tbsp vegan butter
1 nutmeg, grated
6 cups water

Place all ingredients in large pot and bring to a boil. Cook on high heat until sweet potatoes are tender, and water has reduced to form a syrup. Remove from heat and allow to cool. Serve warm.

Cornbread

1 cup yellow corn meal
1 cup cake flour
1/2 cup granulated sugar
1 tbsp plus 1 tsp baking powder
1 tsp salt
1/3 cup canola oil
1 egg equivalent Ener-G Egg replacer
1/2 cup coconut milk
1/2 cup almond milk
2 tbsp soy free Earth Balance, melted
1 tbsp vegetable shortening

Preheat oven to 400°. Place 2 tbsp shortening in a cast iron skillet and place in the oven until oven reaches 400*. If you do not have a cast iron skillet, any 8x8 baking dish will suffice. In a large bowl whisk together corn meal, flour, sugar, baking powder, and salt and set aside. add oil, egg replacer, and milks and stir until combined. Fold in melted butter and set aside. With an oven mitt, pull cast iron skillet, or baking dish from oven and pour the melted shortening into batter and stir. Pour batter in skillet or baking dish, and return to oven to bake for 20-25 minutes, or until a toothpick, when inserted in the center, comes out clean.

Wilted Swiss Chard with Sunflower Kernels

1 bunch of rainbow chard, stems removed and cut into ribbons
1 tsp soy free Earth Balance
1 tsp extra virgin olive oil
1 tbsp white onion, diced
2 tbsp sunflower kernels
salt and pepper to taste
lemon wedge

Add vegan butter and olive oil to a large pan over medium heat. Add diced onion and sauté until onions are tender. Add chard, lemon juice, and sunflower kernels, then season with salt and pepper to taste. Cook for 3 minutes and remove from heat. Serve warm.

Roasted Garlic Mashed Potatoes

1 head of garlic
pinch of salt
1/2 tsp extra virgin olive oil
3 lbs yukon gold potatoes, skin on and cubed
1 cup full fat coconut milk (or more if desired)
4 tbsp vegan butter
1 4 oz bag of fresh baby spinach (optional)
salt and pepper to taste

Preheat oven to 400°. Chop off the top of the bulb of garlic and sprinkle with salt and olive oil. Wrap in foil and place on cookie sheet and roast for 30 - 35 minutes. In a large pot bring potatoes to a boil and cook until tender (appr. 10 to 15 minutes). Drain potatoes and place back in pot over medium to low heat. Using a potato masher, mash potatoes until smooth, add butter, coconut milk and stir. Squeeze the bulb of garlic and add it's contents to the potato mixture along with spinach and allow to cook for an additional 5 minutes. Add salt and pepper to taste. Serve potatoes warm. *note, amount of milk can be adjusted as desired. For a more rustic mash, use less coconut milk, for a creamier consistency, use more coconut milk.

Mexican Roasted Corn on the Cobb

6 ears of fresh corn, in husk
vegan mayo
vegan Parmesan cheese
lemon juice (optional)
cayenne pepper

Preheat oven to 350°. Place corn directly onto rack and roast for 30 minutes or until corn is soft. Remove corn from oven, peel back husks, brush with mayonnaise, then sprinkle with parmesan and cayenne. Serve immediately.

Pan Seared Asparagus

1 bunch of asparagus
1 tsp extra virgin olive oil
salt and pepper to taste
lemon wedges

Place large pot of water on to boil. Trim at least one inch from the bottom of the asparagus, taking care to remove all woody portions. Place asparagus in boiling water and allow to cook for 2 minutes. Remove asparagus from boiling water and transfer to a grill pan or cast iron skillet and grill until semi tender, taking care not to overcook. Asparagus should snap when broken in half. Season with salt and pepper and enjoy. Use lemon wedges to squeeze over asparagus before consuming. *Note, only cook as much asparagus as is going to be eaten in one sitting, as reheating it may cause it to become soggy and unappealing.

Balsamic Glazed Brussels and Cauliflower

1 head cauliflower, broken down into florets
3 cups brussels sprouts, halved
2 tbsp extra virgin olive oil
salt and pepper to taste
balsamic glaze (can be found at your local grocer in the vinegar section)

Preheat oven to 400°. Toss cauliflower, brussels sprouts, olive oil, salt, and pepper in a large bowl to coat. Place on a cookie sheet roast for 25 minutes uncovered. Remove from oven and lightly drizzle with balsamic glaze.

Southern Fried Cabbage

1 head cabbage, cored and sliced
1 yellow onion, sliced
1 tbsp canola oil
1 tsp Seasoned salt
1/2 tsp cracked black pepper
pinch of white sugar

Core and slice cabbage and set aside. In a large pot heat oil over medium heat, add oil, onions, salt and pepper. Cover and allow onions to caramelize, cooking for 10 minutes, stirring every 2-3 minutes to ensure onions do not stick (be patient, it's worth the wait, smile). Add sliced cabbage, toss, and cover. Cook for an additional 5 minutes until cabbage is tender. Season to taste with seasoned salt and cracked black pepper. Serve warm.

Sautéed Collard Greens

1 tbsp canola oil
1 yellow onion, sliced
1 yellow chili pepper, sliced
2 bunches of collards, stems removed and sliced
2 tsp Himalayan sea salt
2 tsp granulated garlic
1 tsp granulated onion
pinch of sugar

In a large pan over medium heat, sauté onions and peppers for 2 minutes. Add greens and seasonings to pan, stir and cover. Cook until greens are just wilted, but still bright green and a bit firm. Serve warm.

Down Home Collards

3 bunches of collard greens, cleaned, stems removed, and cut into ribbons
1 medium white onion, diced
6 yellow chili peppers, diced
2 tbsp canola oil
2 tbsp seasoned salt
2 tbsp granulated garlic
3 tbsp granulated onion
1 packet lipton onion soup mix
4 tbsp vegan worcestershire sauce
3 tbsp distilled vinegar
2 tsp black pepper
2 tsp liquid smoke
3 tbsp sugar
8-10 cups water

In a large stock pot, heat oil over medium-high heat; add onions and peppers and sauté until onions are tender, add greens and remaining ingredients. Stir to combine and cover; allowing greens to cook down. Stir every 20 minutes, working any greens that may be caught on the sides of pot into the liquid. Greens are ready to eat once they are fork tender. Adjust seasonings to taste.
*note: this can also be done in a crock pot. Add all ingredients to a crockpot and allow to cook overnight.

Green Beans and Potatoes

2 tbsp canola oil
1/2 cup yellow onion sliced
6 cups vegetable stock (recipe on pg. ???)
1 large russet potato, peeled and cubed
2 lbs. fresh green beans, snapped
2 tsp seasoned salt
2 tsp granulated onion
1 tsp granulated garlic
1 tsp black pepper
more salt, if needed

In a large pot heat oil over medium heat, add onions and cook for 2-3 minutes. Add potato, vegetable stock, green beans, and the remaining ingredients to pot and bring to a boil. Cook for 15 minutes, or until potatoes and beans are tender.

Roasted Butternut Squash

1 butternut squash, peeled, seeded, and cut into 1-inch cubes
2 tbsp light brown sugar (optional)
1-2 tbsp extra olive oil
1 tsp cinnamon
salt and pepper to taste

Preheat oven to 400°. In a small bowl, combine brown sugar and cinnamon and set aside. Toss butternut squash cubes in olive oil, sprinkle with brown sugar cinnamon mixture, salt, and pepper. Spread cubes evenly across a cookie sheet lined with parchment paper or aluminum foil. Roast for 30 minutes or until squash begins to brown. Serve warm.

Baked Beans

3 cups Great Northern Beans, soaked
4 cups water
1 cup light brown sugar
1/2 cup white onions, diced
1/2 cup molasses
1/4 cup ketchup
2 tbsp yellow mustard

2 tsp liquid smoke
1 tsp salt
1/2 tsp black pepper

Combine all ingredients in a large crock pot, stir to combine, and cook on high for 3 to 4 hours, or until beans are tender.

Greek Grilled Veggies

2 tbsp extra virgin olive oil
2 large red bell peppers
zucchini, sliced to 1/4 inch rounds
yellow squash, sliced to 1/4 inch rounds
eggplant, sliced to 1/4 in thick rounds
Cremini mushroom caps
2 red onions, quartered
1 bunch green onions, trimmed
6-8 flatbreads
1 recipe of hummus (page 16)
1 recipe of tzatziki sauce (page 80)

Place grill pan over medium-high heat. Toss vegetables with olive oil and sprinkle with salt and grill until lightly charred. Grill bell peppers for 2 to 3 minutes, then add the zucchini, squash, eggplant, and mushrooms and grill for another 3 minutes. Add green onions and grill for 3 minutes. Remove veggies from heat and set aside. Place flatbreads on grill for 1-2 minutes until slightly charred. Smear flatbreads with a dab of hummus, top with grilled veggies and tzatziki sauce.

Chickpea Mash and Spinach

4 cups soaked chickpeas (appr. 2 cups dry)
6 cups water, plus more for soaking
2 tsp sea salt
1 tsp granulated onion
1/2 tsp granulated garlic
1/2 tsp black pepper
1/4 tsp nutmeg, grated fresh, if possible
1/4 tsp cinnamon
1 tsp extra virgin olive oil

1/2 tsp minced garlic
1 - 10oz package of chopped frozen spinach, thawed
Salt and pepper to taste

Soak 2 cups of dried chickpeas in water overnight. Be sure to add plenty of liquid to the peas, as they will double in size as they rehydrate. Drain and rinse soaked peas, then add chickpeas, water, and spices to a medium stock pot and bring to a boil, cover and allow chickpeas to cook until done (approximately 45 minutes, chickpeas will have a bit of a crunch to them). Strain chickpeas from liquid and reserve 1 cup of liquid to add to mashed chickpeas. Reserve the remainder of the broth to use as a mock chicken broth for other recipes. Place 4 cups of the chickpeas into a food processor and add 1/4 cup of reserved liquid at a time and blend until smooth; texture should be as that of mashed potatoes. Add 1 tsp of olive oil to the pot over a medium heat, add 1/2 tsp minced garlic and sauté for 2 minutes. Add chickpea mixture, along with remaining whole chickpeas and spinach, and cook for 5 minutes; add salt and pepper to taste. Garnish with freshly grated nutmeg and olive oil and serve immediately.

Daric's Famous Fried Corn
3 tbsp soy free Earth Balance
2 tbsp red bell pepper, diced
2 tbsp green bell pepper, diced
2 yellow chili peppers, diced
1/4 cup white onion, diced
2 sprigs green onion
1 tbsp garlic, minced (2 cloves)
8 ears fresh corn kernels
1 tsp red pepper flakes
1 tbsp granulated garlic
1 tbsp granulated onion
2 tsp cracked black pepper

In a large nonstick pan over medium heat melt butter, then add in bell pepper, chili peppers, onions, and garlic and sauté for 3 minutes. Add in corn and seasonings and continue to sauté for 5-7 minutes, until corn is tender. For a bit of a kick, add in 1/2 tsp of cayenne pepper. Serve warm.

Dessert

PBnC No Bake Brownies

Ingredients

1 cup unsalted roasted peanuts
1 cup walnuts, soaked and rinsed
20 pitted whole dates
1/4 cup raw cacao
1/4 shredded coconut
1-4 tbsp water

*Note, brownies are great when garnished with melted dark chocolate, pictured above.

Directions

1. Soak walnuts in water for 1 hour. Drain, rinse, and set aside.
2. In a food processor pulse peanuts and walnuts until broken down into a paste.
3. Add dates and pulse 10-15 times. Mixture will be a bit lumpy.
4. Add cacao, coconut, and 1 tbsp water and process until smooth.
5. Add more water 1 tbsp at a time until a ball forms.
6. Press mixture into an 8x8 inch glass dish.
7. Freeze for at least 1 hour.
8. Cut into 1 inch squares and serve.

Sweet Potato Pie

5 lbs garnet yams
5 cups granulated sugar
8 eggs (egg replacer)
1.5 whole nutmegs, grated (1 tbsp)
4 oz vegan butter (1/2 cup)

1/2 tsp ground ginger
1/4 tsp cinnamon
2 tsp pure vanilla extract
2 graham cracker pie crusts, 9 inches

1. Preheat oven to 350°
2. Place yams in a large pot and fill with enough water to cover the yams by 2 inches. Boil yams until fork tender and remove from heat.
3. Once yams have cooled enough to handle, peel skins and place yams in a large mixing bowl. Add butter and sugar and combine using a potato masher. Once incorporated, add nutmeg, egg replacer, and remaining spices to mixture. Use a hand blender to break down until mixture is smooth.
4. Pour batter into pie crusts and bake for 1 hour and 15 minutes
5. Remove pies from oven and allow to cool and set before serving.

Chocolate Chip Cookies

Prep Time: 30min | Total Time: 45min | Yields 20 cookies

Ingredients

3/4 cup soy free Earth Balance
2 tbsp non hydrogenated shortening
1 cup light brown sugar
1/2 cup granulated sugar
1 egg - Energy Egg Replacer
2 tbsp apple sauce
1 tbsp molasses
1 tsp vanilla extract
1 1/2 cup whole wheat flour
1/2 tsp salt
1/2 tsp baking soda
1 - 12oz bag of vegan Dark Chocolate Chips

Directions

1. Preheat oven to 325°
2. Melt shortening and vegan butter, add sugars and molasses and beat until color lightens. Add egg replacer and beat for another 50 strokes. Add vanilla and applesauce.
3. In a separate bowl combine flour, salt and baking soda. Add flour mixture to wet ingredients and stir until fully incorporated.
4. Stir in chocolate chips, drop batter onto an ungreased cookie sheet 1 tbsp at a time, and bake at 325 for 12 minutes.
5. Transfer cookies to wire rack and allow to cool, or eat fresh out of the oven.

Dreamy Chocolate Mousse

Prep Time: 10min | Total Time: 5hrs 10min | Serves 6-8

Ingredients

2 cups fresh full fat coconut milk, or one
15 ounce can
20 dates, pitted
1/2 cup raw cashew pieces
1/4 cup raw cacao
2 tsp agave

Directions

1. Place all ingredients in a high
   speed blender and blend on
   highest setting for 2 minutes.
2. Transfer mousse into airtight
   container and refrigerate for at
   least one hour, or until mousse
   sets.

Cookies N Dreamin' Ice Cream

Prep Time: 30min I Total Time: 45min I Serves 8-10

Ingredients

2 cups fresh coconut milk
1 cup fresh almond milk
1 cup granulated sugar
1 tsp pure vanilla extract
1/2 tsp xanthan gum

Mix-In's
8 Oreo cookies, broken

*Note: Be sure to use full fat coconut milk. If using canned product, do NOT use cream of coconut.

Directions

1. Place all ingredients in a high speed blender and blend until smooth and creamy.
2. Transfer mixture to ice cream or gelato maker and prepare according to manufacturer's instructions.
3. Once ice cream has reached soft serve consistency, add mix-in's and churn for 2 minutes.
4. Transfer to an airtight container and freeze until use.
5. Enjoy!

Caramel Mocha Delight

Prep Time: 10min | Total Time: 5hrs 10min | Serves 8-10

Ingredients

3 cups fresh full fat coconut milk
3/4 cup raw sugar
1/2 vanilla bean
1 tbsp ground espresso beans
1/2 tsp xanthan gum

Toppings

vegan caramel sauce
vegan whipped cream
fresh fruit

Directions

1. Place all ingredients in a high speed blender and blend on highest setting for 2 minutes.
2. Transfer mixture into airtight container and refrigerate for one hour.
3. Pour mixture into ice cream or gelato maker and prepare according to manufacturer's instructions.
4. Top and serve.

Prep Time: 45min I Total Time: 2 hrs 15min I Serves 8

Mocha Almond Fudge Pie

Ingredients

Recipe for Mocha Ice Cream on previous page (pg. 59)
1 chocolate wafer pie crust (pg. 76)
[for garnish]
3/4 cup raw fudge (page 76)
1/2 cup slivered almonds (for garnish)

Directions

1. Prepare fudge and pie crust and set aside.
2. Once ice cream has reached the consistency of soft serve, pour into pie crust and spread evenly. Cover with saran and freeze for 45 minutes or until set.
3. When serving, top with warm fudge and slivered almonds.

Creamy Peanut Butter Ice Cream

Ingredients

2 cups fresh full fat coconut milk
1/2 cup organic peanut butter, plus more for mix-ins
1/4 cup light brown sugar, packed
2 tbsp maple syrup
1 tsp pure vanilla extract or 1 whole vanilla bean
1/2 tsp xanthan gum

Mix-in
organic peanut butter

Directions

1. Place all ingredients in a high speed blender and blend on highest setting for 2 minutes.
2. Transfer mixture into airtight container and refrigerate for one hour.
3. Pour mixture into ice cream or gelato maker and prepare according to manufacturer's instructions.
4. Once ice cream reaches soft serve consistency, add in mix-in's.

Strawberries N Cream Ice Cream

Prep Time: 10min | Total Time: 75min | Serves 8-10

Ingredients

1.5 cups coconut milk
1/2 cup almond milk
1/2 cup raw sugar, I used Zulka
1/2 vanilla bean
1/2 tsp xanthan gum
2 cups (1 pint) strawberries quartered
3/4 cup water
3/4 cup granulated sugar
1/2 tsp cornstarch plus 1 tbsp water, combined

Directions

1. Combine first 5 ingredients in a high speed blender and blend for 90 seconds. In a medium sauce pan over medium heat bring water and sugar to a boil, whisk in cornstarch slurry until fully incorporated, then reduce heat, add strawberries, and simmer for 5 minutes until berries soften. Remove from heat and strain liquid from berries into a separate bowl; add liquid and half of the berries to ice cream mixture and combine. Refrigerate mixture for an hour and add to ice cream maker and churn until mixture is of soft serve consistency. Add in berries and churn for an additional 3-5 minutes and serve.

Mango Pineapple Sorbet

Prep Time: 10min | Total Time: 40min | Serves 8-10

Ingredients

3 large mangos, peeled and seeded
1.5 cups pineapple chunks
1 cup purified water
1/2 - 3/4 cup agave or maple syrup
2 tbsp fresh Meyer lemon juice
1/8 tsp xanthan gum

Note - adjust sweetener according to the sweetness of your fruit.

Directions

1. Place all ingredients in a high speed blender and blend on highest setting for 2 minutes.

2. Pour mixture into ice cream or gelato maker and prepare according to manufacturer's instructions.

3. Serve with fresh berries.

Prep Time: 30min I Total Time: 45min I Serves 8-10

Strawberry Sorbet

Ingredients

4 cups strawberries, frozen
3/4 cup agave or simple syrup
1 cup purified water
2 tbsp fresh squeezed Meyer lemon juice

Directions

1. Place all ingredients in a high speed blender and blend on highest setting for 2 minutes.

2. Pour mixture into ice cream or gelato maker and prepare according to manufacturer's instructions.

3. Top with fresh berries and serve.

Very Berry Sorbet

Ingredients

3 cups frozen strawberries
1/2 cup frozen blueberries
1/2 cup frozen blackberries
1/2 - 3/4 cup agave or maple syrup
2 tbsp fresh Meyer lemon juice
1 tsp lemon zest

Directions

1. Place all ingredients in a high speed blender and blend on highest setting for 2 minutes.

2. Pour mixture into ice cream or gelato maker and prepare according to manufacturer's instructions.

3. Top with fresh berries and serve.

Prep Time: 15min | Total Time: 1 hrs 10min | Serves 6-8

Yummy Bread Pudding

Ingredients

8 cups French or Italian bread, cubed
2 cups fresh coconut milk
4 egg equivalent, egg replacer, I used Ener-G
1 cup granulated sugar
1/4 cup brown sugar
1/2 cup golden raisins
2 tbsp vegan butter
1.5 tsp cinnamon
1 tsp pure vanilla extract

Topping
Rum sauce - recipe on page 78

Directions

1. Preheat oven to 350°
2. Cut bread into cubes and drizzle with melted butter, then toss with raisins.
3. In a large bowl whisk together milk, sugars, cinnamon, and vanilla extract.
4. Prepare the egg replacer as directed by manufacturer's instructions, and add to milk mixture.
5. Pour over bread, using the whisk to slightly push down on bread, encouraging it to soak up liquid; let stand for 10 minutes.
6. Bake uncovered for 45 minutes, or until bread is golden on top and springs back when touched. Cut into squares and top with rum sauce and serve warm.

Apple Blueberry Crisp

Filling

8 large rome apples, peeled and cored

1 pint blueberries, rinsed

1.5 tsp cinnamon
1/4 tsp nutmeg
1/8 tsp ground cloves
3 tbsp buckwheat flour
Juice from 2 lemons
1c turbinado sugar
2 tbsp maple syrup
3 tbsp soy free Smart Balance
1/2 cup water

Topping

1 cup rolled oats
3/4 light brown sugar
1/2 cup oat flour
1 cup cold soy free Earth Balance

Directions

1. Place all filling ingredients in a large bowl and toss to coat.
2. In a separate bowl, combine topping ingredients by using the back of a fork to cut through mixture until crumbles form and Earth Balance has been fully incorporated.
3. Spoon topping evenly over apple mixture, bake uncovered for 45-50 minutes, or until apples are tender and mixture is bubbling.

Prep Time: 10min | Total Time: 1hrs 20 min | Serves 8

Prep Time: 30min I Total Time: 45min I Serves 3-4

Boysenberry Cobbler

Ingredients

4 cups boysenberries

1 cup sugar

2 tbsp soy free Earth Balance

1/4 cup all purpose flour

1 cup purified water

1/2 cup fresh squeezed lemon juice

vegan pie crust

Directions

1. Preheat oven to 350°
2. In a large saucepan over medium heat, combine water, lemon juice, and sugar, and cook until sugar dissolves
3. Add berries and reduce heat to a simmer.
4. Add flour and smart balance and cook until mixture begins to thicken (approximately 3 minutes)
5. Remove from heat, pour into ramekins until 3/4 full, and allow mixture to cool.
6. Cover each ramekin with pie crust; cut slits in top of crust so heat can escape while baking
7. Sprinkle crust with sugar
8. Bake at 350° for 20 minutes, or until crust is golden brown.
9. Remove from oven and allow to cool

Marinara Sauce

8 medium tomatoes, peeled, seeded, and diced.
2 tbsp extra virgin olive oil
2 cloves garlic, minced
1 medium red onion, chopped
6 oz tomato paste
1/4 cup dry red wine
1 tbsp sugar
1 tsp dried oregano
3 basil leaves, chopped
1 tsp salt
1/2 tsp cracked black pepper

In large sauce pan, heat oil over medium to high heat and sauté the onions and garlic until onions begin to brown. Add the remaining ingredients and bring to a boil. Reduce heat and simmer until sauce thickens, approximately 35 minutes, stirring occasionally.

Savory Cream Sauce

1 can whole fat coconut milk
1/2 cup almond milk
1 medium yukon gold potato
1 clove garlic
1 tbsp soy free Earth Balance
1 tbsp fresh lemon juice
1 tsp salt or more to taste
1/2 tsp black pepper
1 tsp nutritional yeast

Bring two quarts of water to a boil. Peel and dice potatoes and boil until tender. Place boiled potatoes and remaining ingredients in a high speed blender for 90 seconds. Serve over pasta or use as a dipping sauce for breadsticks.

Bechamel Sauce

5 tbsp vegan butter
1/4 cup flour
4 cups coconut milk
salt and white pepper to taste
1/8 tsp ground nutmeg

In a saucepan on a medium to low heat, warm coconut milk. In a large saucepan over medium heat, melt vegan butter and whisk in flour until smooth. Stir rue continuously with whisk for 5 to 7 minutes or until golden. Add hot coconut milk 1 cup at a time while whisking continuously until all the milk is incorporated. Bring mixture to a boil and add salt to taste and nutmeg. Set aside until ready to use.

Sweet Hoisin Glaze

2 tbsp Hoisin sauce
2 tbsp honey or agave
2 tbsp robust molasses
2 tbsp soy sauce

In a small mixing bowl combine all ingredients. Store in an airtight container and refrigerate until ready for use.

Tzatziki

6 oz plain cultured coconut milk
2 garlic gloves
1 tsp ground cumin
1/2 tsp Himalayan sea salt
1 tbsp fresh lemon juice
1 tsp fresh dill, chopped
1/2 cup shredded cucumber
In a large bowl combine, yogurt, garlic, cumin, sea salt, lemon juice and dill. Stir in cucumber and serve with flat breads and grilled veggies.

Roasted Veggies and Such

Roasted Beets

3-4 medium beets, tops removed
1 tbsp extra virgin olive oil
salt and pepper to taste

Preheat oven to 400°. Rub beet with extra virgin olive oil, and wrap with foil. Place on cookie sheet and bake for approximately 30 minutes or until fork tender. Unwrap and allow to cool. Once beets have cooled, use paper towel and vigorously rub beet until skin is removed. You can dice beets and toss with the raspberry vinaigrette, or enjoy them as is.

Roasted Garlic

3 garlic bulbs
extra virgin olive oil
pinch of salt

Preheat oven to 400°. Slice off the tops of the bulbs to expose garlic cloves. Drizzle tops of cut bulbs with olive oil and sprinkle with salt. Wrap in foil and place on middle rack of oven and allow to roast for 40 minutes. Remove from oven and allow to cool before handling. To extract the yumminess from garlic bulbs, simply squeeze the bulb from the bottom up, and the creamy goodness will begin to exude. You can also peel away cloves as needed and either use as a spread, or mix with your favorite vegan mayo along with some fresh herbs to make the perfect aioli.

Roasted Corn

8 ears of corn, husks on

Preheat oven to 400. Place corn directly onto oven rack and roast for 20 minutes, or until husks dry out. Remove from oven and let cool for 5 minutes before shucking.

Dressings and Vinaigrettes

Balsamic Vinaigrette

1/4 cup balsamic vinegar
1 tbsp prepared mustard
1 tsp honey or other sweetener(optional)
1 tsp oregano
1/2 tsp Himalayan sea salt
1/2 tsp cracked black pepper
1/4 cup extra virgin olive oil

In a mixing bowl whisk together first six ingredients until well incorporated. Slowly drizzle in olive oil while rapidly whisking until emulsion forms.

Creamy Strawberry Lemongrass Vinaigrette

1/2 cup white balsamic vinegar
2 large strawberries, quartered
1/2 inch piece of lemongrass
1/4 cup canola oil
1 tsp granulated sugar
2 tbsp fresh lemon juice
2 tbsp coconut milk
pinch of pepper

In a blender combine all ingredients, with the exception of the coconut milk and pepper. Blend on high for 30 seconds. Pour mixture through a sieve or cheesecloth to strain berries and lemongrass fibers. Whisk in coconut milk and add pepper. Serve chilled

White Balsamic Vinaigrette

1/4 cup white balsamic vinegar
1 tbsp Dijon mustard
1 tsp honey
1/4 cup extra virgin olive oil

Salt and pepper to taste

In a food processor, combine vinegar, dijon mustard, and honey. Pulse ingredients 3-4 times until blended, then turn processor on and slowly add the olive oil until mixture emulsifies. Add salt and pepper to taste.

Raspberry Balsamic Vinaigrette
1/4 cup raspberry balsamic vinegar
1 tbsp dijon mustard
1 tsp honey or other sweetener(optional)
1 tsp oregano
1/2 tsp Himalayan sea salt
1/2 tsp cracked black pepper
1/4 cup extra virgin olive oil

In a mixing bowl whisk together first six ingredients until well incorporated. Slowly drizzle in olive oil while rapidly whisking until emulsion forms.

Citrus Vinaigrette
1/4 cup white balsamic vinegar
juice from one medium lemon
2 tbsp fresh squeezed orange juice
2 tbsp minced shallot
1 tbsp orange zest
1 tbsp honey
1 tsp dijon mustard
pinch of salt
1/4 tsp cracked black pepper
1/3 cup extra virgin olive oil

In a mixing bowl whisk together first six ingredients until well incorporated. Slowly drizzle in olive oil while rapidly whisking until emulsion forms.

Honey Dijon Dressing
2 tbsp dijon mustard

73

2 tbsp fresh squeezed lemon juice

4 tbsp white wine vinegar

2 tbsp honey

1/2 tsp Himalayan sea salt

pinch of cracked black pepper

2 tbsp extra virgin olive oil

In a mixing bowl whisk together first six ingredients until well incorporated. Slowly drizzle in olive oil while rapidly whisking until emulsion forms, or place in blender on high for 60 seconds.

Zesty Italian Dressing

1 cup white wine vinegar

1/2 cup canola oil

1 tbsp minced garlic

1 tbsp granulated sugar

2 tbsp Italian seasoning

Whisk all ingredients together in a large mixing bowl for 2 minutes, or until sugar is dissolved. Store unused portion in an airtight container in the refrigerator. Dressing will separate when stored; shake or agitate before use after storage. Dressing lasts up to one month when properly stored.

Italian Seasoning Mix

1 tablespoon garlic salt
1 tablespoon onion powder
1 tablespoon white sugar
2 tablespoons dried oregano
1 teaspoon ground black pepper
1/4 teaspoon dried thyme
1 teaspoon dried basil
1 tablespoon dried parsley
1/4 teaspoon celery salt
Combine all spices and store in an airtight container, and use as needed.

Creole Seasoning

5 tbsp sweet paprika
3 tbsp Himalayan sea salt or kosher salt
2 tbsp dried oregano
2 tbsp granulated onion
2 tbsp granulated garlic
2 tbsp dried basil
1.5 tbsp dried thyme
1 tbsp cracked black pepper
1 tbsp cayenne pepper
Combine all spices and store in an airtight container, and use as needed.

Taco Seasoning

3 tbsp chili powder
2 tbsp granulated onion
2 tbsp ground cumin
1 tbsp granulated garlic
1 tbsp sweet paprika
1 tbsp sugar

1.5 tsp salt
Combine all spices and store in an airtight container, and use as needed

Pizza Seasoning
1 tsp Himalayan sea salt
2 tbsp dried onion flakes
1/2 tsp dried thyme
1/2 tsp red chili flakes
1/2 tsp granulated garlic
Combine all spices and store in an airtight container, and use as needed.

The Sweeter Things in Life

Dreamy Chocolate Fudge Sauce

3/4 cup coconut oil
3/4 cup light agave
1 cup raw cacao
1 tsp pure vanilla extract

Place all ingredients in a high speed blender and blend for 45 seconds. Pour sauce over your favorite ice cream, or use as a dip for fresh fruit. Place remainder in an airtight container and store in refrigerator for up to one month.

Traditional Pie Crust

2.5 cups all purpose flour, plus more for rolling crust
2.5 tbsp granulated sugar
1/2 tsp salt
8 very cold tbsp Earth Balance
8 very cold tbsp Vegetable shortening
5 tbsp ice cold water

In a food processor, combine flour, sugar, and salt. Add in earth balance and shortening and pulse until mixture becomes a bit crumbly (about 10 pulses). Add 3 tbsp of water, pulsing after each addition, add water 1 tbsp at a time, pulsing after each addition until crust just forms a ball. Remove ball from food processor and immediately wrap in saran, form into a round disk, and place in fridge for 30 minutes prior to use. Be careful not to handle too much with your hands, as the heat from them will begin to break down the fats. After dough has rested, dust a work bench with flour and roll out crust to desired thickness.

Chocolate Pie Crust

20 Oreo cookies, cream centers removed and discarded
5 tbsp melted coconut oil

Preheat oven to 350°

Pulverize cookies in a food processor. Melt coconut oil in microwave and pour in processor while cookies are processing, making cookie crumbs are well moistened. Pour mixture into a 9 inch pan and spread evenly across the bottom, while pushing mixture up the sides of the pan. Once mixture is firmly pressed and spread evenly throughout, place in oven and bake for 5 minutes. Remove pan from oven and allow to cool. Once cooled, pie shell is ready for use.

Vegan Cream Cheese Frosting

1 cup powdered sugar
½ cup non-hydrogenated shortening, cold
2 Tablespoons non-dairy milk
1 teaspoon apple cider vinegar
½ teaspoon vanilla extract
¼ teaspoon lemon juice
¼ teaspoon salt

Place all ingredients in a food processor and process for about 1 minute. Scrape down the sides and process for another minute. The mixture should be smooth and creamy. Store in an airtight container in the refrigerator for up to 2 weeks or in the freezer for up to 6 months. This recipe makes about 2 cups Easy Vegan Cream Cheese Frosting, or enough for about one layer of an 8 inch diameter cake.

Rum Sauce

4 tbsp vegan butter
1 cup light brown sugar
1/2 cup coconut milk
1/4 tsp freshly grated cinnamon
1 capful of rum extract or 3 tbsp Meyer's Rum

In a medium saucepan melt butter, then add in brown sugar and cook on medium-high heat until sugar crystals dissolve. Add in coconut milk, cinnamon, and extract then reduce to a simmer. Spoon sauce over dessert while warm.

Candied Walnuts

1 tbsp raw sugar
1 cup walnut pieces (or nut of your choice)
pinch of salt

Place sugar in a medium saucepan over medium heat until sugar is completely melted. Add walnut pieces and salt, then stir with a wooden spoon until nuts are coated with sugar mixture. Remove from heat and transfer nuts to a piece of parchment paper and allow to cool. Use the back of a spoon to break apart nuts and enjoy.

Simple Syrup

1 cup granulated sugar
1 cup water

In a medium saucepan over high heat, combine water and sugar until sugar is dissolved. Bring to a boil and remove from heat and let cool. Transfer mixture to a glass jar with an airtight lid and refrigerate. Mixture can be stored up to 1 month. This is great to keep around the house to use for mixed drinks, or to quickly sweeten cold drinks like iced tea or lemonade.

Pure Vanilla Extract

2 vanilla beans, split
1 - 1.75 liters of very cheap vodka

Remove cap and splash guard from vodka bottle. Scrape caviar from vanilla bean and add it to vodka. Place split vanilla beans into vodka, replace splashguard and cap and shake vigorously. Wrap bottle in aluminum foil and store in a cool, dark cabinet. Agitate vodka mixture once per day for an entire week, then cut back to once per week. After 3 weeks, you have pure vanilla extract that's great for baking because it does not discolor your food, and it's extremely cost effective.

Fresh Coconut Milk

The meat from one young coconut
2 cups water

Place coconut meat and water in a blender for 60 seconds and blend until mixture is smooth. Pour coconut and water mixture through a cheesecloth to strain. Coconut milk can be stored up to 3 days in the fridge. For vanilla flavored coconut milk, you can add 1/2 tsp of pure vanilla extract to milk after straining. The remaining coconut flakes can be dehydrated and stored for later use, or placed in an airtight container and refrigerated. I sprinkle these goodies over a bowl of granola, or add them to a smoothie for some extra fiber and flavor.

Almond Milk

1 cup raw almonds
2 cups purified water
1 tsp simple syrup

Place all ingredients in a blender or food processor on high for 60 seconds. Using a cheesecloth, strain the pulp and store milk up to 4 days. You can adjust the sweetener up or down if needed, or omit it from the recipe. This should yield about 2 cups of almond milk. You can also add a bit of vanilla extract to spice things up a bit.

Conversion Chart

Unless otherwise noted, all spoon and cup measurements are level. To ensure proper leveling, use the back edge of a butter knife to level off all dry ingredients such as flour, sugar, baking powder, and dry spices. When measuring liquids, it is best to use a clear glass measuring cup. Dry ingredients are best measured by weight; liquid is measured by volume. Use the conversation tables below for reference.

Dry Measures

Cup	Fluid Ounces/ ml	Tablespoons	Teaspoons
1 cup	8oz/ 250ml	16 tablespoons	48 teaspoons
3/4 cup	6oz/ 190ml	12 tablespoons	36 teaspoons
2/3 cup	5oz/ 150ml	11 tablespoons	33 teaspoons
1/2 cup	4oz/ 125ml	8 tablespoons	24 teaspoons
1/3 cup	3oz/ 100ml	5 tablespoons	15 teaspoons
1/4 cup	2oz/ 60ml	4 tablespoons	12 teaspoons
1/8 cup	1oz/ 30ml	2 tablespoons	6 teaspoons
1/16 cup	1/2oz/ 15ml	1 tablespoon	3 teaspoons

Index

Starters

Smoothies

Salads

Salads

Pasta

Sandwiches and Wraps

Entrées

Sides and Small Plates

Green Bean Almondine, 45
Sautéed Spinach, 45
Candied Yams, 45
Fluffy Cornbread, 46
Wilted Swiss Chard with Sunflower Kernels, 46
Roasted Garlic Mashed Potatoes, 47
Mexican Roasted Corn on the Cobb, 47
Pan Seared Asparagus, 47
Balsamic Glazed Brussels and Cauliflower, 48
Southern Fried Cabbage, 48
Sautéed Collard Greens, 49
Down Home Collard Greens, 49
Green Beans and Potatoes, 50
Roasted Butternut Squash, 50
Baked Beans, 50
Greek Grilled Veggies, 51
Chickpea Mash and Spinach, 51
Daric's Famous Fried Corn, 52

Desserts

Chuck's Un-Brownies, 54
Sweet Potato Pie, 55
Chocolate Chip Cookies, 56
Dreamy Chocolate Mousse, 57
Cookies N Dream Ice Cream, 58
Caramel Mocha Delight Ice Cream, 59
Mocha Almond Fudge Pie, 60
Creamy Peanut Butter Ice Cream, 61
Strawberries N Cream, 62
Mango Pineapple Sorbet, 63
Very Berry Sorbet, 64
Yummy Bread Pudding, 65
Apple Blueberry Crisp, 66
Boysenberry Cobbler, 67

Sauces

Roasted Veggies and Such

Dressings and Vinaigrettes

Spice Blends

The Sweeter Things in Life